Kid's Box

Updated
Second Edition

T0384687

Activity Book 1

with Online Resources

British English

Caroline Nixon & Michael Tomlinson

Cambridge University Press
www.cambridge.org/elt

Cambridge Assessment English
www.cambridgeenglish.org

Information on this title: www.cambridge.org/9781316628744

© Cambridge University Press 2008, 2014, 2017

First published 2008
Second edition 2014
Updated second edition 2017

40 39 38 37 36 35 34 33 32 31 30 29 28 27 26 25 24

Printed in Malaysia by Vivar Printing

A catalogue record for this publication is available from the British Library

ISBN 978-1-316-62874-4 Activity Book with Online Resources 1
ISBN 978-1-316-62766-2 Pupil's Book 1
ISBN 978-1-316-62784-6 Teacher's Book 1
ISBN 978-1-316-62894-2 Class Audio CDs 1 (4 CDs)
ISBN 978-1-316-62940-6 Teacher's Resource Book with Online Audio 1
ISBN 978-1-316-62860-7 Flashcards 1
ISBN 978-1-316-62852-2 Language Portfolio 1
ISBN 978-1-316-62972-7 Interactive DVD with Teacher's Booklet 1 (PAL/NTSC)
ISBN 978-1-316-62799-0 Presentation Plus 1
ISBN 978-1-316-62867-6 Posters 1
ISBN 978-1-316-62782-2 Monty's Alphabet Book

Additional resources for this publication at www.cambridge.org/kidsbox

Kid's Box

Activity Book 1

Caroline Nixon & Michael Tomlinson

1 ✏️ Match.

2 🔊 CD1 ✏️ Listen and circle the tick or cross.

3  Look and match.

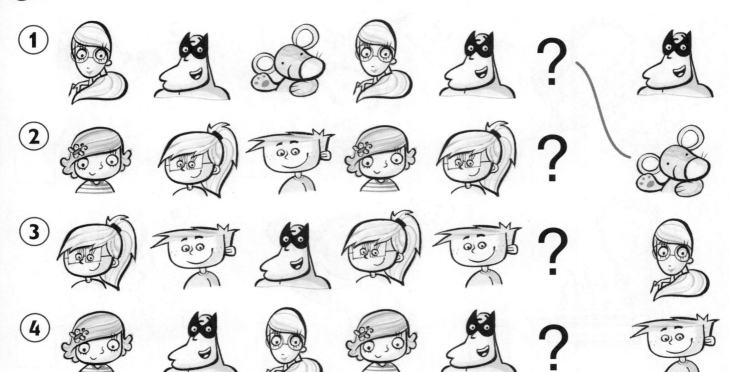

4 Join the dots.

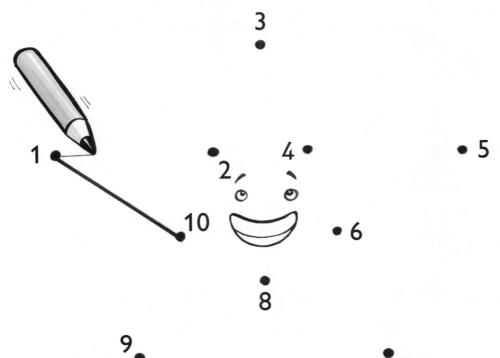

5 🔊 ✏️ **Listen and write the number.**

① ② 6 ③

④ ⑤ ⑥

6 ✏️ **Draw and write.**

Me!

I'm _____Stella_____ .
I'm _____seven_____ .

Me!

I'm _____ .
I'm _____ .

Listen and colour.

8 🔊 **15** CD1 ✏️ Listen and circle the 's' words.

9 🔊 **16** CD1 ✏️ Listen and tick (✓) the box.

My picture dictionary ⭐⭐

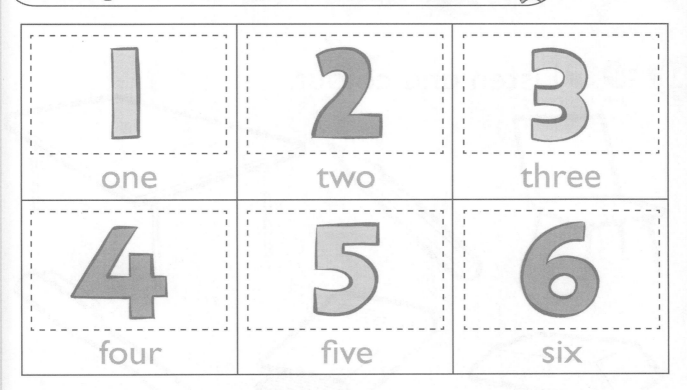

1 one	2 two	3 three
four	five	six
4	5	6

My star card ⭐⭐

 Can you say these words?

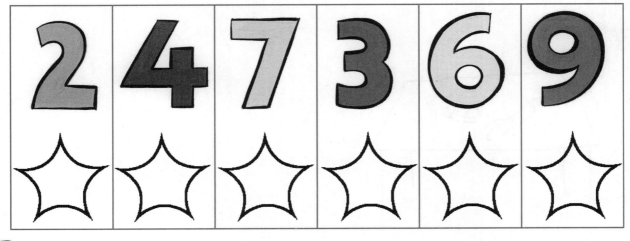

2 4 7 3 6 9

✏️ Colour the stars.

1 21 CD1 Listen and colour.

2 Draw your table.

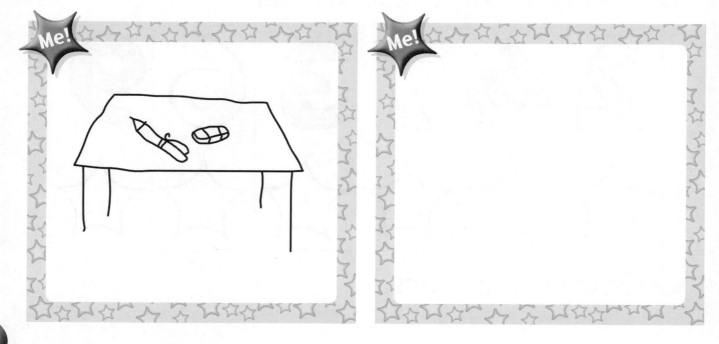

3 ✏️ Draw three pictures.

①	②	③

💬 ✏️ Now tell your friend.
Draw your friend's pictures.

Number one is a chair.

④	⑤	⑥

4 ✏️ Count. Write the number.

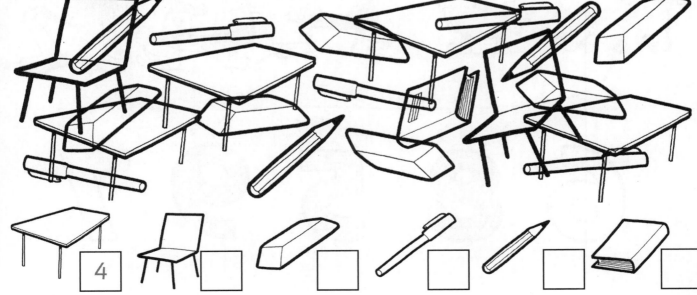

4

5 🎧26 CD1 ✏️ Listen and write the number.

6

6 ✏️💬 Match and answer.

6 8 5 9 7

7 🔍✏️ Look and read. Put a tick (✓) or a cross (✗).

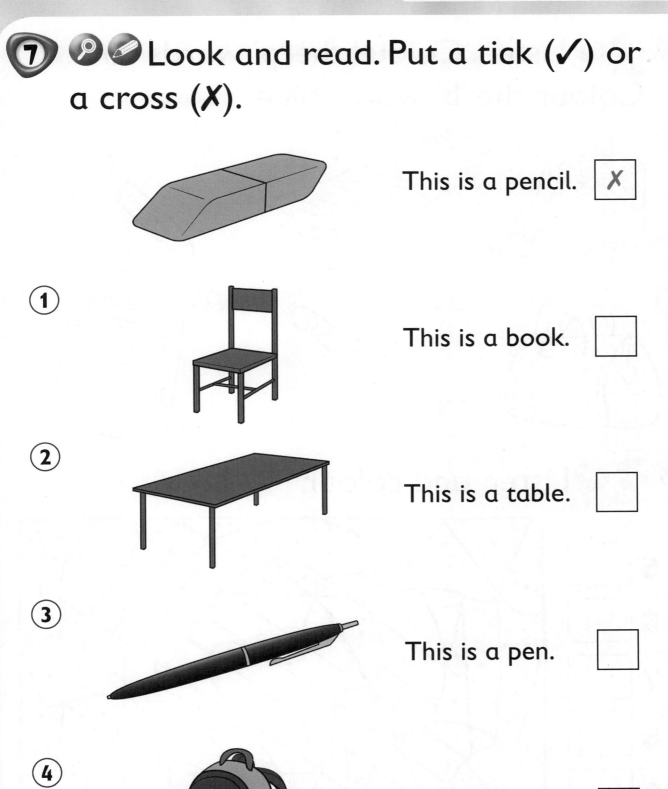

This is a pencil. ☒

1 This is a book. ☐

2 This is a table. ☐

3 This is a pen. ☐

4 This is a bag. ☐

8 🔊 **CD1 30** ✏️ Listen. Colour the 'p' words pink. Colour the 'b' words blue.

9 🔊 **CD1 31** ✏️ Listen and colour.

5
6
7
8
9
10

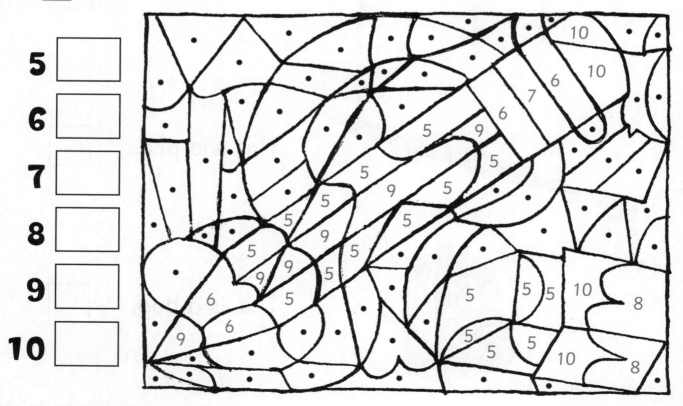

My picture dictionary

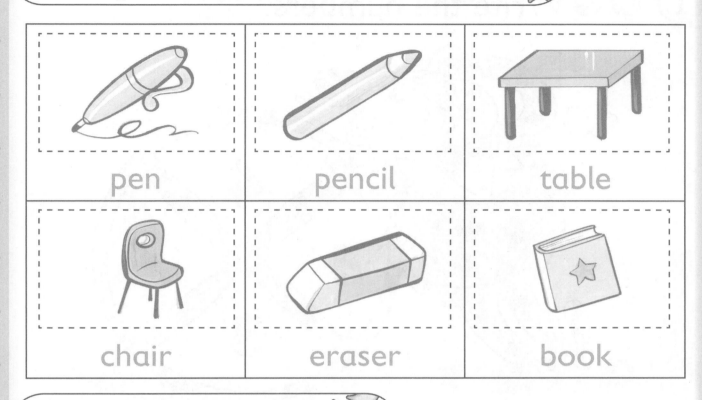

pen

pencil

table

chair

eraser

book

My star card

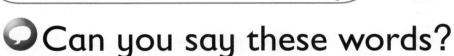

Can you say these words?

Colour the stars.

Now you! **1** 🔍 ✏️ Write the numbers.

① 1 + 4 = ⎯5⎯   ② 4 + 1 = ⎯⎯⎯

③ 3 + 2 = ⎯⎯⎯   ④ 2 + 3 = ⎯⎯⎯

⑤ 4 + 3 = ⎯⎯⎯   ⑥ 3 + 4 = ⎯⎯⎯

2 💬 ✏️ Write and answer. Say.

① ⎯3⎯ + ⎯2⎯ = ⎯5⎯

② ⎯⎯⎯ + ⎯⎯⎯ = ⎯⎯⎯

③ ⎯⎯⎯ + ⎯⎯⎯ = ⎯⎯⎯

④ ⎯⎯⎯ + ⎯⎯⎯ = ⎯⎯⎯

What are three and two?

Five.

3 💬 ✏️ Ask two friends and write.
Then draw and colour.

What's your name?   How old are you?

I'm _____Sam_____ .
I'm _____seven_____ .

I'm _____ .
I'm _____ .

I'm _____ .
I'm _____ .

1 Listen and circle the tick or cross.

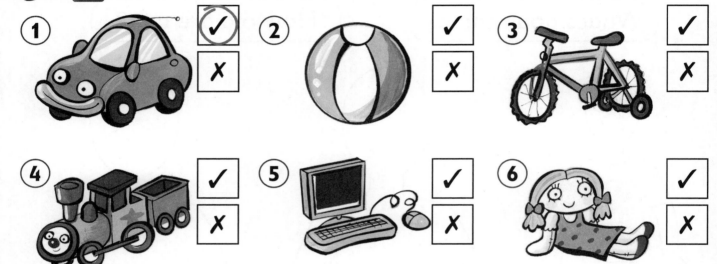

2 Look and complete.

3  Listen and draw coloured lines.

① ② ③ ④ ⑤ ⑥

4 Colour the toys.

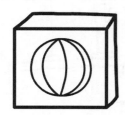   

Now ask and answer. Colour your friend's toys.

What colour's your ball?   It's white.

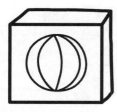   

5 🎵 44 CD1 ✏️ **Listen and write the number.**

6 🔍 ✏️ **Look and circle.**

7   Listen and draw lines.

Matt   Alice   Hugo

Eva   Mark   Mary

8 🔊 49 CD1 ✏️ Listen and circle 't' or 'd'.

① **t** d

② t d

③ t d

④ t d

⑤ t d

⑥ t d

⑦ t d

⑧ t d

9 🔊 50 CD1 ✏️ Listen and colour.

My picture dictionary

car

ball

bike

train

doll

computer

My star card

Can you say these words?

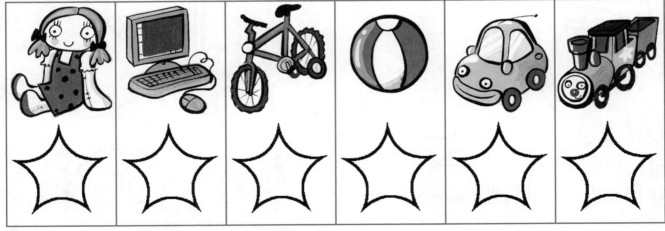

Colour the stars.

4 My family

1 💬 ✏️ **Who is it? Match and answer.**

2 🔊 ✏️ **Listen and colour.**

This is my family.

3 🔊⁷ CD2 ✏️ **Listen and draw coloured lines.**

4 ✏️ **Draw your family.**

Me!

5 Listen and colour the stars.

This is my family.

6 Circle and say.

She's beautiful.

1
2
3
4
5
6

7  Look and complete the words.

 <u>b</u>eautiful

 u e i b u t a f l

(1)  ___ld

 o d l

(2)  ___ad

 d s a

(3)  ___gly

 u l y g

(4)  ___appy

 p p h a y

(5)  ___oung

 u n y o g

8 🎧16 CD2 ✏️ Listen and circle the 'a' in the words.

1. c(a)t

2. s a d

3. b a g

4. h a p p y

5. f a m i l y

6. b l a c k

9 🎧17 CD2 ✏️ Listen and write the number.

1

My picture dictionary

grandfather   grandmother   mother

father   brother   sister

My star card

Can you say these words?

Colour the stars.

Marie's art — Mixing colours

 Read and colour. Write.

| g | r | e | e | n |

| o | r | a | n | g | e |

| p | u | r | p | l | e |

| p | i | n | k |

~~| g | r | e | y |~~

1 + = | g | r | e | y |

white + black

2 + = red + white

3 + = blue + yellow

4 + = red + yellow

5 + = blue + red

30

2 🔍 ✏️ Draw and complete the pictures.

Review

1 🔊 24 CD2 ✏️ Listen and join the dots.

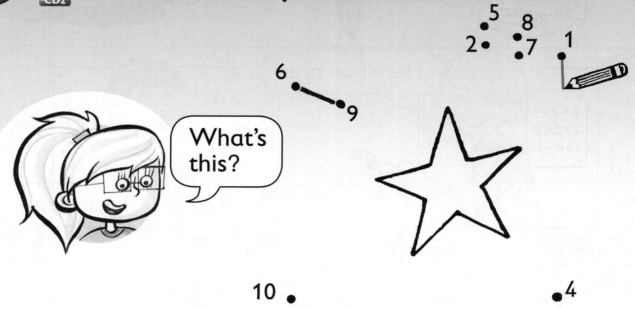

What's this?

5
8
2
7
1
6
9
10
3
4

2 🔍 ✏️ Look and draw.

3 🔍✏️ **Count and write the number.**

6					

4 💬🔍 **Say, look and answer.**

Two, pencil.

He's ugly!

5 Our pets

1 🔊28 CD2 ✏️ **Listen and circle the tick or cross.**

2 🔍 ✏️ **Look and write the words.**

| a bird | a cat | a dog | a fish | a horse | ~~a mouse~~ |

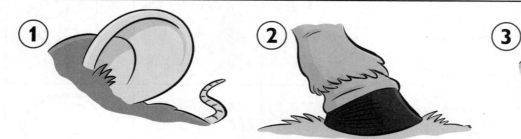
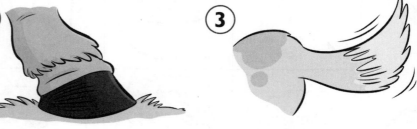

① a mouse

② _____

③ _____

④ _____

⑤ _____

⑥ _____

3 ✏️ Colour the pets.

💬✏️ Now ask and answer. Colour your friend's pets.

What colour is the fish?   It's blue.

4 💬✏️ Read and answer.

| birds   fish   ~~mice~~   cats   horses |

① What are they? They're _____ .

② What are they? They're _____ .

③ What are they? They're _____ mice _____ .

④ What are they? They're _____ .

⑤ What are they? They're _____ .

5 🔍 ✏️ Read and circle.

① short / (long)

② clean / dirty

③ small / big

④ short / long

⑤ big / small

⑥ clean / dirty

6 🔊33 CD2 ✏️ Listen and follow.

7 🔍✏️Look and read. Put a tick (✓) or a cross (✗).

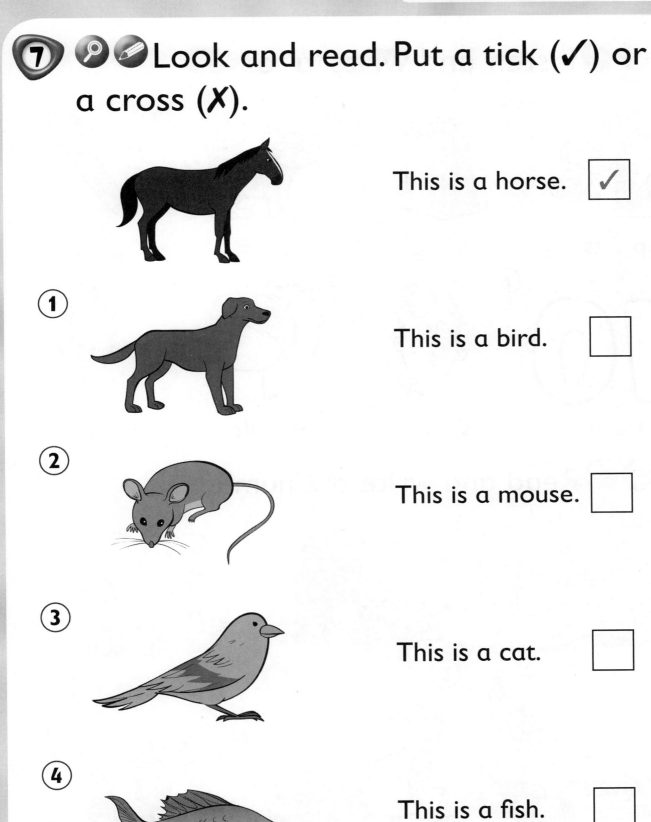

This is a horse. ✓

1 This is a bird. ☐

2 This is a mouse. ☐

3 This is a cat. ☐

4 This is a fish. ☐

8 CD2 38 ✏️ Listen and write 'a' or 'e'.

1. p_e_ts
2. b__g
3. c__t
4. p__n
5. t__n
6. s__d
7. St__lla
8. h__ppy

9 🔍 ✏️ Read and write the number.

a dirty dog [3]   a big dog [ ]   two short dogs [ ]

a long dog [ ]   three small dogs [ ]   a clean dog [ ]

My picture dictionary

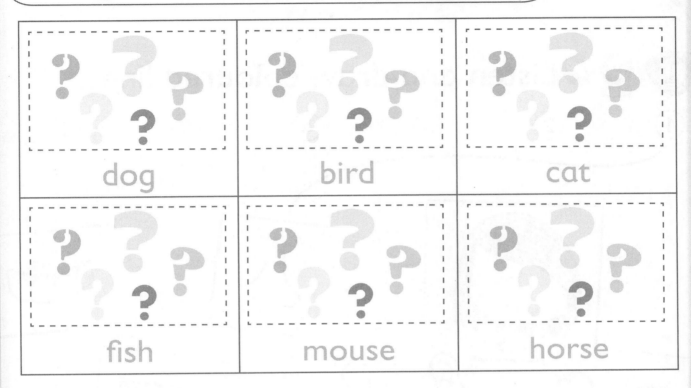

dog

bird

cat

fish

mouse

horse

My star card

Can you say these words?

Colour the stars.

6 My face

1 🔊42 CD2 ✏️ Listen and draw coloured lines.

① ② ③ ④ ⑤ ⑥

2 ✏️ Circle the different word.

①	bike	(nose)	train	doll
②	table	horse	mouse	bird
③	eyes	ears	teeth	ball
④	book	pen	car	pencil
⑤	fish	horse	cat	head
⑥	dog	four	ten	seven

3 **45** **CD2** 🖊 **Listen and write the number.**

4 🖊 **Write the words.**

| e | a | r | s | | e | y | e | s | | h | a | i | r | | m | o | u | t | h |

| n | o | s | e | | | | | | | | | | | | t | e | e | t | h |

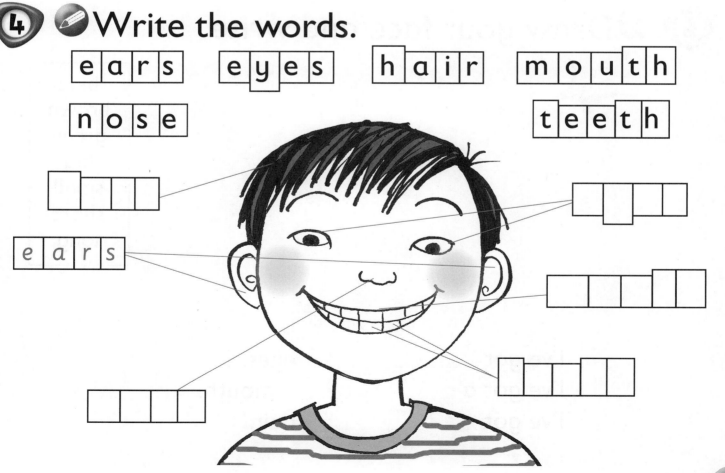

Listen and draw. Listen and colour.

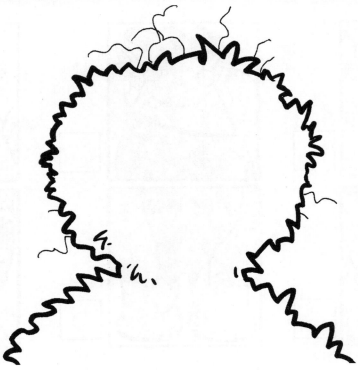

6 **Draw your face and write.**

Me!

| blue |
| brown |
| green |
| big |
| small |
| short |
| long |

I've got _____ eyes.

I've got a _____ mouth.

I've got _____ hair.

Read and write.

A monster

I'm a happy monster. My __head__ is very big. I've got long

black (1) _____ . I've got three (2) _____ .

On my face, my (3) _____ is small, but I haven't got

a small mouth. In my mouth, I've got big (4) _____ .

I've got a pet. My pet is a (5) _____ .

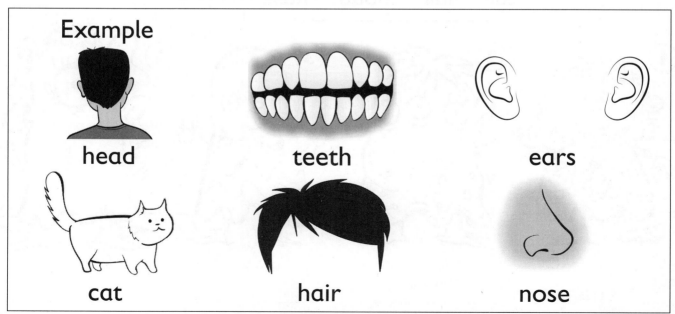

Example

head   teeth   ears

cat   hair   nose

8 🔊52 CD2 ✏️ **Listen and complete the words.**

① f r og

② ___ ___own

③ ___ ___aw

④ ___ ___een

⑤ ___ ___other

⑥ ___ ___ain

9 🔊53 CD2 ✏️ **Listen, look and draw. Write.**

| ~~eye~~ hair mouth nose |

① eye ②___ ③___ ④___

My picture dictionary ⭐⭐

ears   eyes   mouth

nose   hair   teeth

My star card ⭐⭐

 Can you say these words?

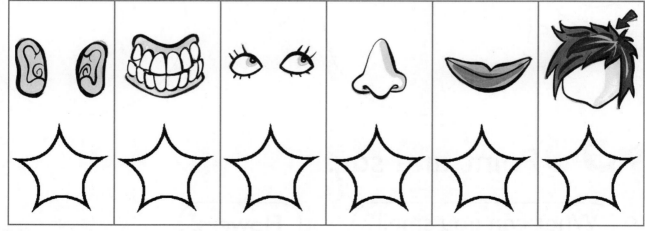

Colour the stars.

Marie's science — The senses

Now you! **1** ✏️ Look and write. Find and draw.

1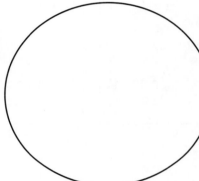

hear

taste
touch
~~hear~~
see
smell

2

- - - - - - - - - -

3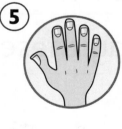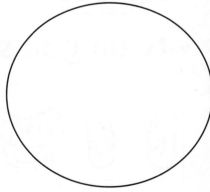

- - - - - - - - - -

4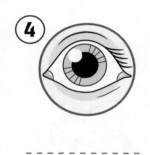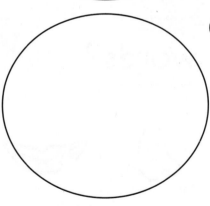

- - - - - - - - - -

5

- - - - - - - - - -

2 👂💬 Point and say.

What can you smell?   Flowers.

46

3 Read and match.

1

2

I brush my cat.

I wash my horse.

I feed my fish.

I walk my dog.

3

4

4 Draw and write.

Me!

| brush |
| feed |
| wash |
| walk |

This is my _____ . I _____

and _____ my _____ .

7 Wild animals

1 🔊 ✏️ Listen and join the dots.

2 ✏️ Read and draw lines. ↓ ↘ →

①

~~doll~~	~~bike~~	~~ball~~
nine	hippo	bag
table	seven	eight

②

elephant	ten	crocodile
chair	seven	car
computer	five	bag

③

pencil	ball	bag
tiger	eraser	one
doll	five	book

④

bike	two	door
three	doll	train
snake	monkey	giraffe

3 Read and answer. Write 'yes' or 'no'.

1 Are the giraffes sad? ...no..

2 Are the elephants happy? ....

3 Are the crocodiles long? ....

4 Are the snakes short? ....

4 Colour the animals.

Now ask and answer. Colour your friend's animals.

My giraffes are purple.

⑤ ▶**9** 🖊 Listen and write the number.

| | | | | 1 |

⑥ 🔍🖊 Read and cross (**✗**) or tick (**✓**).

Animals	hands	arms	legs	feet	tails
snakes	✗	✗	✗	✗	✓
monkeys					
birds					
elephants					
crocodiles					
fish					
tigers					
zebras					

7 🔍✏️ Look and read. Write 'yes' or 'no'.

The elephants have got small ears.   no

1 The monkeys are on bikes.   _____

2 The giraffes are under the elephants.   _____

3 The small giraffe is fat.   _____

4 The tigers are next to the crocodiles.   _____

5 The snakes have got eyes.   _____

8 🔊 ✏️ Listen and write 'a', 'e' or 'i'.

1. l_e_g

2. f__sh

3. bl__ck

4. b__g

5. h__ppo

6. p__n

7. s__ster

8. h__nd

9 ✏️ Draw and write.

Me!

My favourite wild animals are _____.
They're _____.
They've got _____.

52

My picture dictionary

crocodile | elephant | tiger

hippo | giraffe | snake

My star card

 Can you say these words?

Colour the stars.

1 🔍 ✏️ Find and circle the number.

🧦	1	2	3	4	5	6	7	8	9	(10)
👕	1	2	3	4	5	6	7	8	9	10
👗	1	2	3	4	5	6	7	8	9	10
👟	1	2	3	4	5	6	7	8	9	10
🧥	1	2	3	4	5	6	7	8	9	10
👖	1	2	3	4	5	6	7	8	9	10

2 🔊 17 CD3 💬 Listen and answer.

3  **20 CD3** Listen and colour.

4 Draw and write.

Me!

My favourite clothes are my _____.

5 **23** **CD3** ✏️ Listen and colour.

Sue

Nick

Kim

Tony

May

6 **24** **CD3** ✏️ Listen and match.

7 Read the question. Listen and write a name or a number. There are two examples.

| 3 | ~~Kim~~ | Tom | ~~10~~ | 8 | Bill | 9 |

What is the name of the girl?   _____ Kim _____

How old is she?   _____ 10 _____

① What is the name of the dog?   _____

② How old is the dog?   _____

③ What is the name of Kim's brother?   _____

④ How old is Kim's brother?   _____

⑤ How many children are in Kim's class?   _____

8 Listen and write 'a', 'e', 'i' or 'o'.

① d _o_ ll

② c __ p

③ d __ g

④ p __ n

⑤ f __ sh

⑥ s __ ck

⑦ b __ x

⑧ s __ x

9 Write the sentences.

① an orange | She's got | skirt.

She's got an orange skirt.

② jacket. | a blue | He's got

③ They've got | shorts. | white

My picture dictionary

jacket

shoes

skirt

socks

trousers

T-shirt

My star card

 Can you say these words?

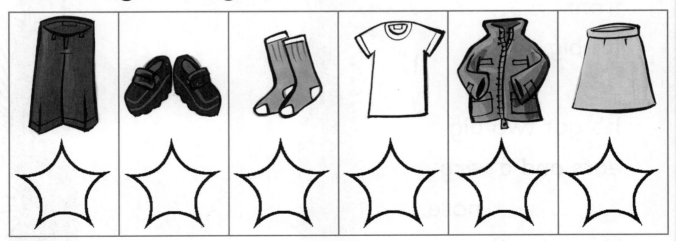

Colour the stars.

1 🔍✏️ **Read and tick (✔) or cross (✗).**

	river	plain	forest
fish 🐟	✔	✗	✗
giraffe			
hippo			
crocodile			

 **2** 🔍✏️ **Read. Write and draw.**

~~plains~~ long grey elephant forests

This animal is from

_____plains_____ and

from _____ .

It's big and

_____ .

It's got two big

ears and a very

_____ nose.

What is it? It's an

_____ .

60

3 🖊 **Read and write the number.**

① The birds are sad. `4`

② The river is dirty. ☐

③ The forest has got trees. ☐

④ The river hasn't got fish. ☐

⑤ The forest hasn't got trees. ☐

⑥ The birds are happy. ☐

⑦ The river has got fish. ☐

⑧ The river is clean. ☐

1 🔍 ✏️ Read, draw and colour.

Ben

Bill

Bill
long shoes
a dirty T-shirt
a big nose
a sad mouth
purple trousers

Ben
short shoes
a happy mouth
green hair
a small nose
a red jacket

2 37 CD3 💬 Listen and say 'Bill' or 'Ben'.

3 💬 Say the sentences.

Fish and snakes haven't got legs.

	and		
fish	and	snakes	no legs.
cats	and	dogs	no hands.
zebras	and	giraffes	no arms.
elephants	and	crocodiles	no hair.

4 🔍✏️ Read and write.

arms   ears   ~~face~~   hands   mouth   tail   two   two

At the safari park

I'm small and brown. I've got a funny ① _face_

2

with ② _____ big ③ _____ and a big

④ _____ . My ⑤ _____ are long and

2

I've got ⑥ _____

big ⑦ _____ . I've got

a long ⑧ _____ .

1 🎵40 CD3 ✏️ **Listen and write the number.**

2 🔍 ✏️ **Read and match.**

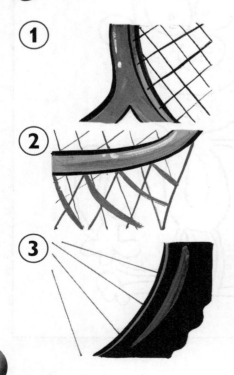

swim
play the guitar
play tennis
ride a bike
play football
play basketball

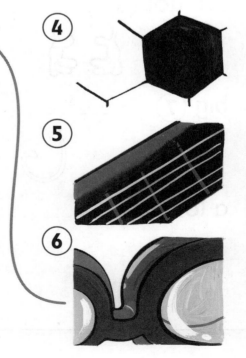

3 🔍✏️ Find six words.

① [?] a [?]

③ [?]

② [?] [?]

④ play the [?]

```
w  a  s  g  r  i  d  e
r  s  p  u  g  i  t  a
a  w  b  i  k  e  r  p
t  i  n  t  i  s  l  l
o  m  l  a  s  t  c  a
o  m  e  r  x  u  r  y
t  e  n  n  i  s  a  e
```

4 ✏️ Write the words.

①  ②  ③  ④  ⑤  ⑥

football ~~guitar~~ play ride swim tennis

① play the __guitar__   ④ play _____

② _____ basketball   ⑤ _____ a bike

③ play _____   ⑥ _____

5 🔊 46 CD3 ✏️ Listen and tick (✓) or cross (✗).

① ✗   ② ☐   ③ ☐

④ ☐   ⑤ ☐   ⑥ ☐

6 ✏️ What can you do? Draw and write.

Me! ✓

✗

✓

✗

I can _____
_____
_____ .

I can't _____
_____
_____ .

7 Look and write the words.

Example

_b a s k e t b a l l_

b s k a t e
b l l a

Questions

1

_ _ _

r c a

2

_ _ _ _

k i b e

3

_ _ _ _ _

r s h o e

4

_ _ _ _ _ _

n i n e t s

5

_ _ _ _ _ _

t a g u i r

8 Listen and circle 'l' in the words.

1 Lily

2 blue

3 football

4 pencil

5 play

6 clean

7 yellow

8 plane

9 Write the words.

| basketball a bike draw football the guitar |
| a horse the piano sing swim tennis |

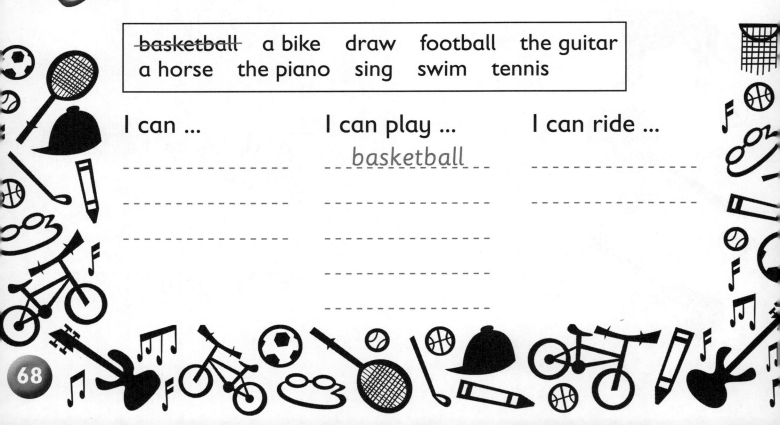

I can ...

I can play ...
basketball

I can ride ...

My picture dictionary

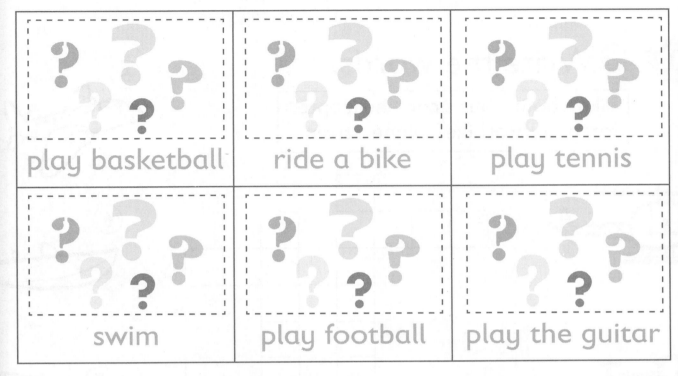

play basketball | ride a bike | play tennis

swim | play football | play the guitar

My star card

 Can you say these words?

Colour the stars.

10 At the funfair

1 ✏️ Write the words.

bike boat bus car ~~helicopter~~
lorry motorbike plane train

①

②

③

⑤

⑥

⑦

⑧

Crossword:

1 down: h e l i c o p t e r

④

⑨

2 🔊 CD4 ✏️ Listen and colour.

3 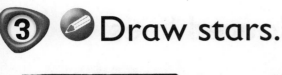 Draw stars.

   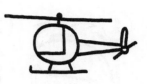

Now ask and answer. Draw your friend's stars.

> Where's the star?

> It's on the lorry.

   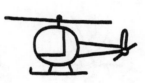

4 Write the words.

~~lorry~~	~~T-shirt~~	helicopter	boat	trousers	~~plane~~
skirt	jacket	shoes	motorbike	socks	bus

lorry

T-shirt

5 **9** CD4 ✏ Listen and draw coloured lines.

6 ✏ Draw and write.

| riding | horse | bike | motorbike | driving | sitting |
| lorry | bus | ship | flying | plane | helicopter |

Me!

I'm _____ a _____ .

7 **Listen and tick (✓) the box. There is one example.**

Where's the lorry?

 **A** ✓
 **B**
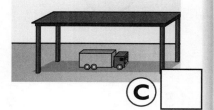 **C**

1 What is Anna doing?

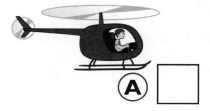 **A**
 **B**
 **C**

2 What toy is under the chair?

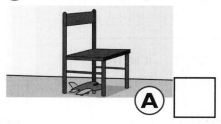 **A**
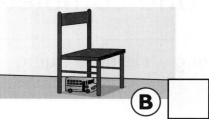 **B**
 **C**

3 What colour is Matt's motorbike?

 **A**
 **B**
 **C**

4 Which boy is Alex?

 **A**
 **B**
 **C**

8 🔵15 ✏️ Listen and write 'a', 'e', 'i', 'o' or 'u'.

① h_a_ppy

② s___cks

③ b___s

④ s___ng

⑤ d___ck

⑥ f___sh

⑦ s___d

⑧ l___g

9 🔍✏️ Read and complete.

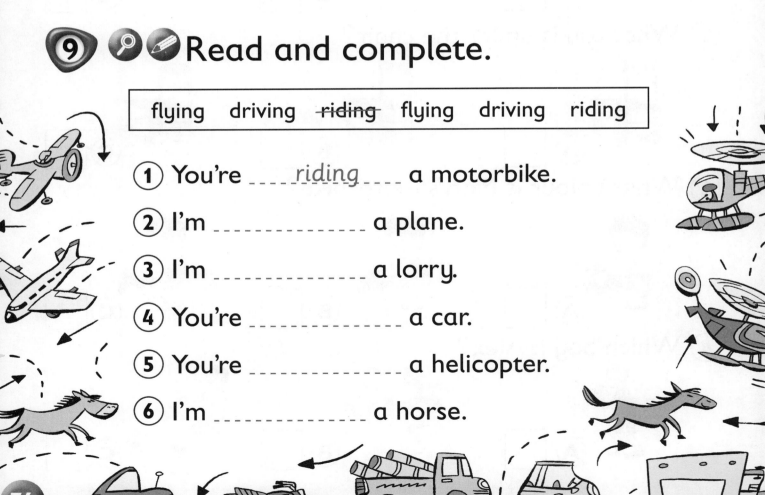

| flying | driving | ~~riding~~ | flying | driving | riding |

① You're ____riding____ a motorbike.

② I'm _____ a plane.

③ I'm _____ a lorry.

④ You're _____ a car.

⑤ You're _____ a helicopter.

⑥ I'm _____ a horse.

My picture dictionary

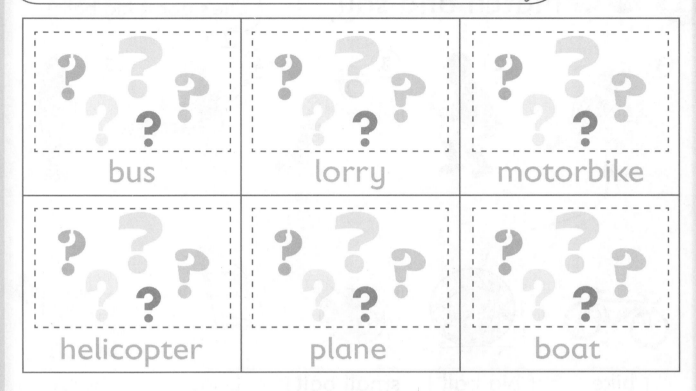

bus

lorry

motorbike

helicopter

plane

boat

My star card

Can you say these words?

Colour the stars.

Now you! **1**  Match and say.

She's got a big ball.

①  ② ③ ④ ⑤

bike   big ball   small ball   boat   horse

2 Match and write.

horse   boat   basketball   ~~bike~~   table-tennis

① They're riding a .... *bike* ....

② They're sitting on a ....

③ They're playing ....

④ They're playing ....

⑤ They're riding a ....

3 💬✏️ Work in teams. Colour the boxes.

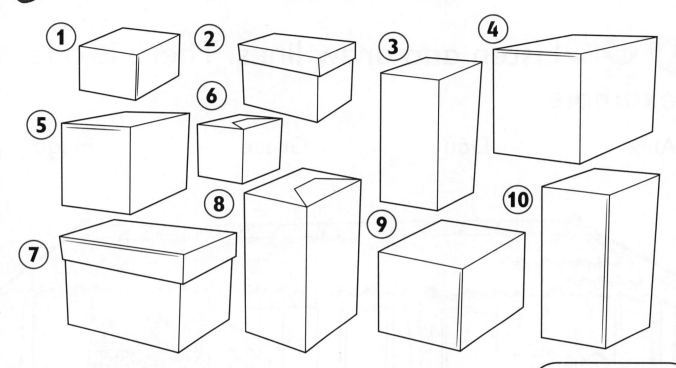

4 🧒✏️ Play the game in teams.

Number one is yellow.

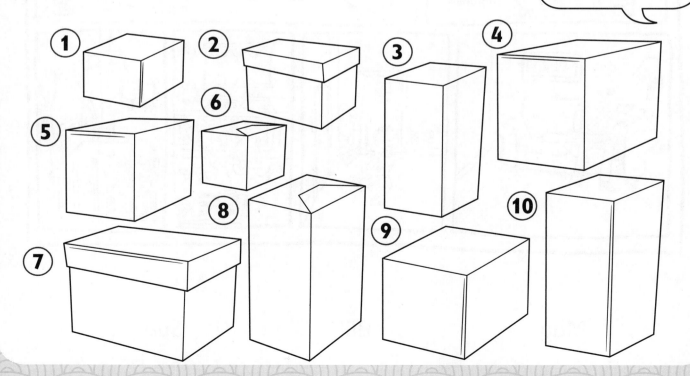

Our house

1 🎧 23 CD4 ✏️ Listen and draw lines. There is one example.

Alex   Dan   Grace   Hugo

May   Bill   Sue

② 🔍✏️ **Follow the lines and write.**

| ~~bedroom~~ | living room | kitchen | hall |

① ② ③ ④

bedroom ....

③ ✏️ **Draw your house.**

Me!

My house has got

....
....
....
....
....
....
....

4 🔊 28 CD4 ✏️ Listen and colour the stars.

5 🔍 ✏️ Match and write.

(1) She's drawing a _____picture_____ .

(2) He's reading a _____ .

(3) She's sitting on a _____ .

(4) They're listening to _____ .

(5) He's driving a _____ .

(6) They're playing _____ .

 chair

 tennis

 car

 book

 music

 picture

6  **Look, read and write.**

Where are the children?   in the .... kitchen ....

How many people are there?   .... two ....

①What's the girl eating?   some ....

②What's the boy got?   a ....

③What's the girl doing?   listening to ....

④What animal can the boy see? an ....

⑤Who is pointing?   the ....

7 🔵 Listen and circle the 'h' words.

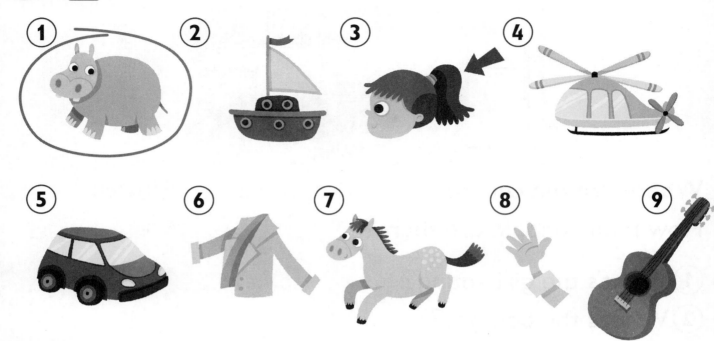

① ② ③ ④ ⑤ ⑥ ⑦ ⑧ ⑨

8 🖊️ Complete the sentences.

eating	~~listening~~	reading	having

① He's __listening__ to music. ② She's _____ a bath.

③ He's _____ a fish. ④ She's _____ a book.

82

My picture dictionary

living room

bedroom

kitchen

bathroom

hall

dining room

My star card

 Can you say these words?

Colour the stars.

1 🔊 37 CD4 ✏️ **Listen and colour.**

2 ✏️ **Circle and write the words.**

a	w	e	i	f	i	s	h	s
c	h	o	c	o	l	a	t	e
a	b	r	e	c	k	f	a	m
k	l	t	c	h	e	j	p	r
e	b	u	r	g	e	r	p	o
p	r	o	e	v	i	s	l	b
b	a	n	a	n	a	t	e	g
j	z	o	m	e	r	s	t	u
o	r	a	n	g	e	v	i	e

 ① _____

 ② _____

 ③ _____

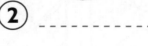 ④ _____

 ⑤ _____

 ⑥ _ice cream_

 ⑦ _____

 ⑧ _____

3  **Write the words.**

① → _____cat_____

② →

③ →

④ →

4 **Read and complete.**

| young |
| ~~eating~~ |
| banana |
| cake |

The small monkey's ___eating___ an orange and the big
monkey's got some _____ .The old monkey's eating a
_____ and the _____ monkey's got ice cream.

5 **42** CD4 ✏ Listen and tick (✔) or cross (✗).

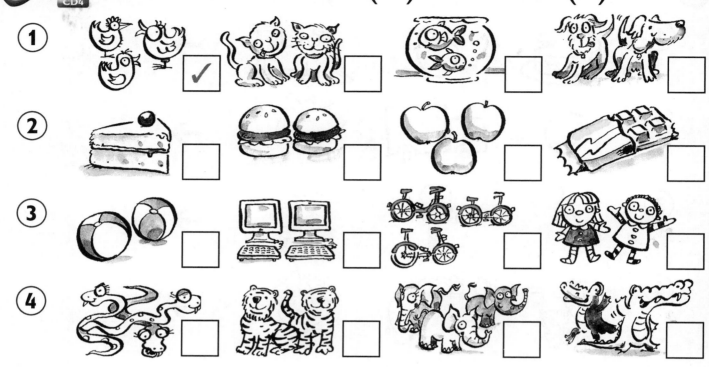

6 ✏ Write 'like' or 'don't like'.

Me!

I _ _ _ _ _ _ _ _ _ _ fish.

Me!

I _ _ _ _ _ _ _ _ _ _ burgers.

Me!

I _ _ _ _ _ _ _ _ _ _ ice cream.

Me!

I _ _ _ _ _ _ _ _ _ _ apples.

Listen and colour. There is one example.

8   Listen and write the words.

| bike | white | drive | nine | ~~like~~ | five |

①
like

② 5

③
_____

④ 9
_____

⑤
_____

⑥
_____

9 Tick (✓) the boxes.

Name	🍎	🍌		🐟	🥧	🍔
Me						

Now ask and answer in groups.

Do you like apples?   Yes, I do.

88

My picture dictionary

apple

banana

burger

cake

chocolate

ice cream

My star card

Can you say these words?

Colour the stars.

1   **Read and circle a word.**

This is Fred Food.

His nose is a banana / an ice cream.

His mouth is a fish / a burger.

His ears are apples / oranges.

His hair is grapes / kiwis.

His eyes are cakes / burgers.

Now you! **2**   **Draw and colour your Fred Food.**

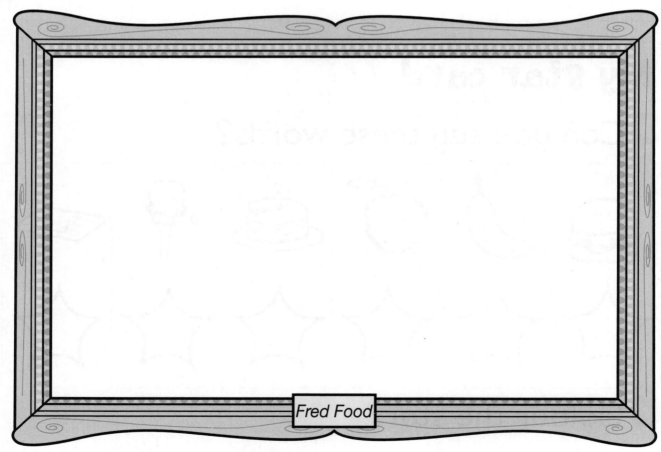

Fred Food

3 🔍✏️ Order the pictures.

① 2 3 1

②

③

4 🔍✏️ Read and write.

| cleaning washing washing |

He's _____
his hands.

She's _____
her teeth.

He's _____
his apples.

Review

1 ✎ Tick (✓) a box.

reading a book						
eating fish						
watching TV						
having a bath						

💬✎ Now ask and answer. Tick (✓) your friend's box.

> What's the old monster doing?

> He's eating fish.

reading a book						
eating fish						
watching TV						
having a bath						

2 ✏️ Circle the different word.

1. kiwi   apple   orange   (guitar)

2. lorry   ice cream   train   bus

3. burger   tiger   giraffe   lion

4. bathroom   kitchen   bedroom   chocolate

5. motorbike   helicopter   lorry   hall

6. play   swim   bike   ride

3 🔍✏️ Read and complete. Draw.

I'm _____ .

I'm at home in
the kitchen. I like

_____ ,

but I don't like

_____ .

My favourite food is

_____ .

Me!

Grammar reference

1 Order the words.

① (your) (name?) (What's) _____

② (old) (are) (you?) (How) _____

2 Look and complete.

| He's   She's   He's   She's |

① _____ Simon. _____ six.

② _____ Stella. _____ seven.

3 Look and complete.

| Is   Is   is   isn't |

① _____ your ball in your car?   Yes, it _____ .

② _____ your ball on the table?   No, it _____ .

4 Circle the sentences.

Wearen'tsad.We'rehappy.Arewebeautiful?

5 Look and complete.

It's	They're

1. Look at the dog. _____ long.
2. Look at the two cats. _____ small

6 Order the words.

1. face. · got · I've · a clean _____

2. You've · short hair. · got _____

7 Circle the sentences.

They'vegottails.Theyhaven'tgothair.Havetheygotlegs?

8 Look and complete.

hasn't got	's got

1. ✓ He _____ your red trousers.
2. ✗ He _____ your red trousers.

9 Order the words.

1. (can) (sing.) (He) ------------------

2. (They) (swim.) (can't) ------------------

3. (Can) (ride a bike?) (you) ------------------

10 Look and complete.

| am   not   Are   Are |

1. _____ you flying your plane?   Yes, I _____ .

2. _____ you playing the guitar?   No, I'm _____ .

11 Circle the sentences.

What'shedoing?Heishavingabath.Ishereading?

12 Look and complete.

| like   don't like |

1. ☺ I _____ cake.

2. ☹ I _____ ice cream.